Sensational Chocolate

A Celebrity Collaboration

Paul A Young

Photography by Lisa Linder

CLEARVIEW

CLEARVIEW

Published in 2016 by Clearview Books
22 Clarendon Gardens,
London W9 1AZ
www.clearviewbooks.com

A CIP record of this book is available
from the British Library.
ISBN: 978-1908337 – 344

Editor: **Catharine Snow**
Food Styling: **Camilla Baynham**
Design: **Lucy Gowans**
Production: **Simonne Waud**

Printed in Europe
Colour reproduction by
XY Digital, London

Special thanks go to Eric Ladd and the
team at XY Digital for providing all
pre-press work on this title for free.

Sensational Chocolate

A Celebrity Collaboration

Paul A Young

CLEARVIEW

CONTENTS

Introduction

I think I must have the best job in the world and I'll tell you why. Two years ago I received an invitation to a charity event from Andy Williamson (Chief Executive of The Children's Air Ambulance). It was so personal, dynamic and remarkable that I gladly accepted it. To my surprise, I spent a hugely enjoyable evening packed with entertainment and brimming with dedication, generosity and humanity.

Being very used to, and highly tuned in with the particular skills of creative people, Andy and his team enabled me to make full use of my Chocolatier's training to feed, entertain and raise funds for a desperately needed second air ambulance helicopter. Yes, second! We only have one for the entire UK, which shook me to the core. 'Why is it we only have one?' I kept asking. A year later and I'm honoured to become an Ambassador for the charity, a very proud ambassador, and it is truly a fantastic job to be able to combine good chocolate with good works...

So this is why Sensational Chocolate was conceived – I thought, why not ask lots of lovely Celebrity supporters, well-known Chefs and friends to donate their favourite chocolate recipes, and put them into a book that would continue to help raise funds for that second helicopter. Then I thought, I'll develop some brand new recipes of my own and put them in too. Not only is chocolate one of the very few foods that is universally adored, children absolutely love it and most of these recipes are ones they can try themselves - or help lick the spoon.

Added to which, chocolate makes us smile, it makes us happy, it feeds our soul and satisfies our cravings which is why the recipes in my book cover all the food groups. It's also the perfect gift for any occasion - a thank you, a sorry, a Happy Birthday, an I love you. All the profits from this book are going back into the charity, and it greatly warms my heart that funds from the sale of my book will keep a trickle or tidal wave of money to help.

I want you to enjoy my book thoroughly, it's a great read, it looks amazing on your coffee table and will become part of your kitchen cookbook library as you enjoy making some of your favourite celebrity and chef recipes.

Paul.a.Young
www.paulayoung.co.uk

The Children's Air Ambulance

The Children's Air Ambulance provides an inter hospital transfer service for critically ill children. The helicopter serves as a flying intensive care unit for babies and children. It is the only helicopter in the country dedicated to doing this and is specifically designed to carry all the things a clinician needs to keep an infant alive on their journey.

The Children's Air Ambulance flies children who are critically ill. They are suffering from serious, and often life threatening illness. They might need heart surgery, not be able to breathe properly, be suffering a life-threatening allergic reaction, need brain surgery, be a cancer patient, or be suffering septicaemia. Children are not always flown to the nearest paediatric intensive care unit, but to the hospital that is the best treatment centre for their condition.

A transfer by helicopter is around four times faster than by road. Children are transported on a specialist stretcher that the charity developed. It took over a year to take the stretcher through aviation approval and there are only seven in existence.

The Children's Air Ambulance flew their first patient in May 2013. Since then they've made over 200 transfers. They've visited 77 different hospitals in England, Ireland, Scotland and Wales, and work with seven specialist NHS paediatric transport teams. An estimated 600 children a year could benefit from the service.

Each transfer costs on average £2,800, but the service is free of charge to patients and the NHS.

They do not receive any government funding.

www.childrensairambulance.org.uk

I was seven maybe eight years old when I baked my first cake in an Aga at my Grandma's house with my Mum. It had two temperatures, incinerate or slow bake, so I became a pretty confident cake baker from an early age. It proved valuable training for my pastry chef years with Marco Pierre White.

A home-baked version of anything beats the mass-produced hands down. It's so easy to have the ingredients sitting in your store cupboard ready to hand, and the smell of chocolate baking as it wafts through your home is better than the smell of bread or freshly made coffee. Nothing can match a great chocolate cake, pudding or biscuit and the secret is all in the chocolate you use. Always try to buy the best quality you can find, but you can also have fun with flavoured chocolate bars – like chocolate orange which I LOVE, LOVE, LOVE. So get baking and have fun!

Cakes, Bakes, Cookies & Biscuits

Marmalade and Prune Chocolate Cake

Sue Foster
Winner of the Children's Air Ambulance chocolate recipe competition

Serves: 8

Preparation time: 25 minutes

Cooking time: 1 hour

You will need: a 20cm springform or loose bottom cake tin.

INGREDIENTS FOR THE CAKE:

125g/4.5 oz/ 1 cup soft pitted prunes

50 ml / 1.7 fl oz brandy

I tsp cinnamon

I tsp mixed spice

240g / 8.5oz / 2 cups plain (all purpose) flour

3 tbps cocoa powder

3 tsps baking powder

½ teaspoon bicarbonate of soda

100g/3.5 oz unsalted (sweet) butter

70g/3.5 oz/ ⅓ cup 70% dark chocolate or chocolate chips

250g / 9 oz / I cup dark brown muscovado sugar

2 large eggs beaten

1 cup single cream

125ml /4 fl oz/ ½ cup Seville orange marmalade

I tsp vanilla extract

2 tsps instant coffee dissolved in 1 tablespoon water

INGREDIENTS FOR CAKE TOPPING:

2 more tablespoons of marmalade

8 tablespoons icing sugar

Put prunes into a small bowl and cover with brandy, mix in cinnamon and spice. Leave overnight

Put prunes, marmalade, coffee mixture, vanilla extract in food blender and blend together until nearly smooth

Sieve flour, cocoa, baking powder, bicarbonate of soda into a bowl, mix in the sugar

Melt the butter then melt the chocolate

Leave the chocolate and butter to cool a little

Mix together the chocolate, butter, eggs, cream, and the blended prune mixture

Make a well in the flour mixture, pour in the wet ingredients: chocolate, butter, eggs, cream, prunes

Fold together and ensure all ingredients are mixed in thoroughly

Cook for 1 hour at Gas Mark 4/180 C/160 C Fan/350 F.

While hot, prick with a skewer, warm 2 tablespoons marmalade until runny and spoon over the cake

Drizzle over the top with glace icing made with icing sugar mixed with hot water

Paul's tip:

Substitute orange marmalade for ginger preserve or lemon marmalade for a vibrant zingy cake.

Anise Infused Lava Cake

Atul Kochhar
Michelin starred Indian chef , restaurateur

Serves: 6

Preparation time: 30 minutes

Cooking time: 30-45 minutes in the fridge then 5 minutes in the oven

You will need: 6 x 6oz pudding moulds

110g unsalted butter

150g dark 70% chocolate

150g sugar

4 medium eggs

50g plain flour

¼ teaspoon ground anise powder

Whisk the eggs and sugar together with an electric handwhisk, until light and fluffy.

Melt the butter and chocolate in a heat proof bowl over a saucepan of simmering water until melted. Let it cool for a few minutes then carefully add in the egg mixture and mix until smooth.

Finally fold in the flour and anise powder, and stir until smooth.

Pour the mixture into pudding moulds until ¾ full and let them cool and set in the fridge for 30-45 minutes.

Pre-heat the oven at 180 C / Gas Mark 4 and bake for 5 minutes.

To serve, turn the puddings out onto plates, and garnish with fresh berries and a scoop of vanilla icecream.

Paul's tip:

If you don't like anise then try cinnamon and nutmeg for a warming festive feel.

Malted Milk and Hazelnut Chocolate Cake

Eleanor Nutt
Children's Air Ambulance fundraiser

Serves: 8-10

Preparation time: 20 minutes

Cooking time: 25-30 minutes

You will need: 2x 20cm round sandwich tins, greased and lined with baking paper

---

INGREDIENTS FOR THE CAKE:

30g malted chocolate drink powder such as Horlicks or Ovaltine

30g cocoa powder

225g butter, softened, plus extra for greasing

225g caster sugar

150g self raising flour

75g ground hazelnuts

4 eggs

1 tsp baking powder

INGREDIENTS FOR THE ICING:

3 tbsp malted chocolate drink powder

1 ½ tbsp hot milk

125g butter, softened

250g icing sugar, plus extra for dusting

50g dark 70% chocolate, melted

1 tbsp boiling water

About 20 Maltesers, to decorate

A handful of crushed hazelnuts, to decorate

Measure the malted chocolate drink powder and cocoa powder into a large bowl, pour over 2 tablespoons of water and mix to a paste. Add the remaining cake ingredients and beat until smooth.

Divide evenly between the prepared tins and bake in the oven for 20–25 minutes. Set aside in the tins to cool for 5 minutes, then turn out on to a wire rack to cool completely.

To make the icing, measure the malted chocolate drink powder into a bowl, add the hot milk and mix until smooth. Add the butter, icing sugar and melted chocolate and mix again until smooth, then add the boiling water to give a gloss to the icing.

Place one cake on a plate and spread over half the icing. Sandwich with the other cake and spread (or pipe) the remaining icing on top, using the tip of a rounded palette knife to create a swirled effect from the centre to the edge of the cake. Arrange the Maltesers over the top, sprinkle with the crushed hazelnuts and dust with icing sugar before serving.

Paul's tip:

Try adding milk chocolate chunks to the mix and a spoon of hazelnut chocolate spread to the icing for a pimped up version.

Chocolate Cake with Chocolate sauce

Giorgio Locatelli
Michelin starred Italian chef, restaurateur

Serves: 8

Preparation time: 45 minutes

Cooking time: 25 minutes

You will need: 20cm round cake tin, baking paper

Butter a 20cm round cake tin (7.5cm deep) and line the base. Preheat the oven to fan 150C/conventional 170C/ gas 4.

Sieve the flour and the cocoa powder together in a bowl. In another bowl mix the eggs and the sugar together and then cook in bain marie (or place the bowl over a saucepan of simmering water) until it reaches 55 degrees. Remove from the heat and place the mixture into a Magimix, KitchenAid or electric handwhisk and beat while it cools, to develop a thick creamy consistency.

INGREDIENTS FOR THE CHOCOLATE SPONGE:

140g self raising flour

20g cocoa powder

4 large eggs

160g caster sugar

40g unsalted butter

Remove $\frac{1}{3}$ of the egg & sugar mixture into a third bowl and mix in the soft butter with a spatula. Into the remaining $\frac{2}{3}$ egg & sugar mixture, add the sieved flour and the cocoa powder.

Combine both mixtures together, folding carefully, and pour it into the cake tin. Cook for 10-15 minutes.

If you push a skewer in the centre it should come out clean and the top should feel firm.

Leave to cool in the tin, then turn out onto a wire rack to cool completely.

INGREDIENTS FOR THE CHOCOLATE SAUCE:

270g caster sugar

215 ml water

80g cocoa powder

140g 70% dark chocolate grated

85g single cream

Bring the water and sugar to the boil in a saucepan, until the sugar has dissolved and the water is clear. Add the cocoa powder bit by bit until it's incorporated, remove from the stove, add the grated chocolate and mix until the chocolate has melted. Stir in the cream and put the entire mixture through a fine sieve. Let it cool down in the fridge until ready to use.

INGREDIENTS FOR THE SYRUP:

250ml water

150g caster sugar

30ml whole milk

30g cocoa powder

Paul's tip:

simply use different origin and percentage chocolate to transform this cake and sauce each time you make it.

In a saucepan bring the water and sugar to the boil until the sugar has dissolved and the water is clear, then let it rest until cold and stir in the milk and the cocoa powder.

Cut the sponge in half and brush syrup on both sides of the sponge. Using a spatula, cover the bottom half of the sponge with chocolate sauce. Put the top half of the sponge over it, then then cover the outside of the cake with the chocolate sauce, letting it fall down the sides and smoothing to cover with a palette knife. Decorate with grated chocolate or a pile of chocolate curls.

(You may have extra syrup and chocolate sauce left over. These can keep in the fridge for up to a week, or can be used as extra sauce for the cake).

Flourless Chocolate Cake

Milly Johnson
Bestselling fiction author

Serves: 8

Preparation time: 45 minutes

Cooking time: 30-40 minutes

You will need: a 23cm shallow flan or tart tin

---

200 g of dark chocolate eg 70% (the higher the cocoa solids the better)

100 g caster sugar

100 g soft brown sugar

200 g butter, cut into cubes for easy melting

5 eggs

½ teaspoon salt

splash of Grand Marnier (optional!)

Pre-heat oven 160°C/320°F/ Gas mark 3

Separate the eggs. Whisk the egg yolks until pale and thick. Whisk the egg whites to the stiff peak stage.

Melt the chocolate, salt and the butter together slowly over a pan of hot water.

As soon as it has melted quickly stir in the sugar and the egg yolks (and the Grand Marnier if used) before the chocolate mix starts to set. Then slowly fold in the egg whites.

Pour into a greased and lined shallow flan dish (23cm/8") (It won't rise much!)

Bake for between 30-40 minutes until the top is slightly crunchy but the middle is still a little gooey.

Leave the cake to cool completely in the tin.

For the orange free version: serve with plain clotted cream and a few raspberries.

For the orange version: serve with double cream flavoured with Grand Marnier and dark chocolate shavings.

Paul's tip:

grate an orange and lemon into the mix for a St Clements spin on this classic recipe.

Sachertorte

Fay Ripley
Actress, cookery writer

Serves: 6-8

Preparation time: 45 minutes

Cooking time: 35 minutes

You will need: a 20-22cm springform cake tin

INGREDIENTS FOR THE CAKE:

200g 70% dark chocolate, broken up

160g butter, softened

120g caster sugar

4 large free-range eggs, separated

200g ground almonds

INGREDIENTS FOR THE ICING:

100g 70% dark chocolate, broken up

50g butter

3 heaped tbsp apricot jam

Preheat oven to 150°c (fan), 170°c, gas mark 6. Line the base of a 20-22cm springform cake tin with baking parchment. Melt the chocolate in a glass bowl set over a pan of simmering water, then set aside.

Using an electric whisk, cream the butter and sugar together till fluffy. Add the egg yolks, melted chocolate and ground almonds and mix until evenly combined.

In a separate bowl, whisk the egg whites with an electric whisk till soft peaks form, then carefully fold into the cake mix. Pop in the tin and bake for 35 minutes, then cool completely in the tin.

For the topping, melt the chocolate and butter in a glass bowl set over a pan of simmering water. Leave to cool slightly.

Carefully remove the cool cake from its tin, then spread the jam over the top of the cake. Dribble over the warm chocolate topping, letting it drip down the sides a little and leave it to set. Serve at room temperature.

This cake is dense and rich and could last a while (if you can avoid the temptation of eating it at every opportunity).

Paul's tip:

*don't mess with this baby...
it's a classic and should not be
changed.*

Chocolate Biscuit Cake

(which others call Fridge Cake)

Jasmine Birtles

Finance expert, TV presenter

Serves: 16-20

Preparation time: 25 minutes

Chilling time: 1 hour

You will need: 20cm round or square baking tin

INGREDIENTS FOR THE CAKE:

340g (12oz) butter

240g (8oz) golden syrup
(v important!)

60g (2oz) unsweetened cocoa
powder

120g (4oz) dark chocolate,
chopped

650g (1.2lb) digestive biscuits (or
any old biscuits that have gone a
bit soft and you don't know what
to do with them)

INGREDIENTS FOR THE TOPPING:

300g (11oz) melted dark chocolate

Put all the biscuits into a strong plastic bag (or two bags for safety) hold the bag with one hand and enjoy yourself for a few minutes bashing the biscuits with a rolling pin until they're crushed up. Watch the bag as it could split if you're too vigorous (n.b. kids love doing this bit).

At the same time, melt the butter, syrup, chocolate and cocoa powder in a pan. Then pour the biscuit mixture into the pan and stir until completely coated. Pour the whole mixture into a 20cm (8in) round or square tin (square is probably best) and press down the mixture to go into all the corners and be as even as possible.

Stick it into the fridge to cool and solidify. When it is set, melt the dark chocolate for the topping and spread evenly over the biscuit mixture. You can also decorate with Maltesers, white chocolate hearts or gold baubles.

You can also replace some of the biscuits with cherries and dried fruit or with pistachios or other nuts.

Paul's tip:

*be creative with your biscuit
choice and mix them up with
different flavours and types.
The options are endless.*

Fruited Chocolate Christmas Cake

Josceline Dimbleby
Cookery writer, journalist

Serves: 16

Preparation time: 1 hour

Cooking time: 1 ½ hours

You will need: A deep 9 inch/23cm round cake tin

---

6 oz (175 g) dried pineapple pieces

6 oz (175 g) dark cooking chocolate

4 oz (125 g) unsalted butter, plus extra for greasing

5 oz (150 g) soft dark brown sugar

4 large eggs (size 1-2), beaten

5 oz (150 g) self-raising flour

2 tablespoons (2 x 15 ml spoons) cocoa

3 oz (75 g) ground almonds

5 tablespoons (5 x 15 ml spoons) brandy or rum

2 teaspoons (2 x 5 ml spoons) ground cinnamon

4 oz (125 g) soft pitted prunes, chopped roughly

4 oz (125 g) crystallized ginger, chopped roughly

4 oz (125 g) walnuts, chopped roughly

4 oz (125 g) candied peel

6 oz (175 g) raisins

coarsely grated rind of 2 lemons

Put the dried pineapple into a bowl, pour over plenty of boiling water and leave for 15–30 minutes and then drain. Line the base of a deep, 9-inch (23 cm) round cake tin with a piece of well buttered greaseproof paper. Line the sides with a wide strip of buttered paper which comes up above the edges of the tin.

Melt the chocolate in a bowl over hot water. Cream the butter and the brown sugar in a mixing bowl, add the melted chocolate and whisk thoroughly until smooth, paler in colour and fluffy. Add the beaten eggs a little at a time, whisking well after each addition. Then sift the flour and cocoa into the bowl and fold them in with a large metal spoon. Fold in the ground almonds, the brandy and the cinnamon. Then fold in the chopped prunes, ginger, walnuts, the candied peel, the raisins and the grated lemon rind. Lastly stir in the soaked pineapple pieces.

Spoon the mixture into the lined cake tin and level the top. Heat the oven to Gas Mark 3/325°F/170°C and bake the cake in the centre for one hour; then turn down to Gas Mark 1/275°F/140°C for 1¼–1½ hours until a knife stuck in the centre comes out clean. Leave the cake in the tin for 10-15 minutes and then take it out of the tin and leave it on a rack to cool. When cold, wrap well in several layers of cling film and store in a cool place until you are ready to ice it.

Paul's tip:

feel free to change the fruits to suit you and add handfuls of nuts and chocolate chunks to really make this a cake to remember.

Whole Cherry Brownies

John Whaite
Winner Great British Bakeoff 2012, author, TV presenter

Serves: 16

Preparation time: 30 minutes

Cooking time: 30-40 minutes

You will need: some paperclips, 20 cm square cake tin, greased and lined

---

16 pitted cherries with stalks left on (see instructions below)

200g dark chocolate

200g salted butter

3 medium eggs

265g caster sugar

150g plain flour

100g white chocolate chips

100g dark chocolate chips

To pit the cherries, take a paperclip and unbend it leaving the hook shaped part as a hook. Insert that hook up into the base of a cherry. Feel the way around the stone – it helps to imagine you're shaving the stone with the paperclip. Gently manipulate out the stone, being careful not to squash the cherry or remove too much flesh. Place them wound side down onto a paper towel.

Preheat the over to 200C/180C fan. To make the brownie batter place the chocolate and butter into a saucepan and set over a low heat. Stirring constantly, melt them together until very smooth and shiny. Remove from the heat and add the eggs and beat in until smooth, then beat in the sugar until it is more or less dissolved. Sift over the flour and fold in along with the chocolate chips until you have an evenly smooth batter. Pour the batter into the prepared tin and bake for 15 minutes.

Remove from the oven and press the cherries into the mixture as evenly spaced as possibly, leaving their tops and stalks poking out. Return to the oven and bake for a final 15 minutes. When ready, the brownie should be a cracked, paler brown on top, and dark brown, dense and gooey underneath. Allow to cool until completely cold, then chill in the fridge before cutting – this just helps to achieve an even, neater cut.

Paul's tip:

I've substituted the cherries for raspberries and blackberries with fantastic results, so dare to be different.

Double Baked
Chocolate Meringue Brownie

Éric Lanlard
French patissier, TV presenter

Serves: 8

Preparation time: 25 minutes

Cooking time: 1 hour 10 minutes

You will need: a 22cm (8½in) diameter springform cake tin, baking paper

---

INGREDIENTS FOR THE BROWNIE:

250g/ 8oz unsalted (sweet) butter, plus extra for greasing

350g / 12 oz / 2 cups 70% dark chocolate, roughly chopped or chocolate chips

300g /10oz/ 1 ½ cups light muscovado sugar

5 large eggs, separated

INGREDIENTS FOR THE CHOCOLATE MERINGUE:

4 egg whites

225g / 7½oz / 1 cup golden caster sugar

2 tsp vanilla extract

1 tsp cornflour

50g/2oz/ ½ cup pure cocoa powder

Paul's tip:

Excellent made in advance and served at room temperature with a glass of dessert wine or Maderia.

Preheat the oven to 180°C (fan 160°C)/350°F/gas mark 4. Grease a 22cm (8½in) diameter springform cake tin and line with baking paper, making sure it is at least 5cm (2in) above the rim of the tin.

To make the brownie, melt the butter and chocolate together in a heatproof bowl set over a saucepan of barely simmering water, making sure the surface of the water does not touch the bowl. Add the sugar, stirring until it has completely dissolved. Remove from the heat and add the egg yolks.

In a clean, dry bowl, whisk the egg whites to soft peaks. Fold a couple of tablespoons of the egg whites into the chocolate mixture, then fold in the remaining whites using a rubber spatula. Spoon the mixture into the prepared tin and bake in the oven for 40 minutes.

Meanwhile, make the meringue. In a large, clean, dry bowl, whisk the egg whites to stiff peaks, adding the sugar a little at a time, then add the vanilla extract. Sift the cornflour and cocoa powder together, then fold into the meringue until the mixture is even and glossy.

Remove the chocolate brownie from the oven and cover the top with the meringue. Return to the oven for a further 25 minutes, or until the meringue puffs up and a crust forms on the top but the centre is still soft. Leave to cool in the tin. The centre will collapse slightly.

Serve warm, decorated with grated chocolate and crème fraîche or vanilla ice cream.

Pistachio and Chocolate Shortbread

Edd Kimber
Winner Great British Bakeoff 2010, author, TV presenter

Makes: around 24 biscuits

Preparation time: 15 minutes

Cooking time: 25-30 minutes

You will need: two baking trays lined with parchment paper, electric whisk.

100g/3.5 oz / ½ cup unrefined golden caster sugar

200g/ 7 oz unsalted (sweet) butter, room temperature

Zest of 1 lemon

275g / 10 oz/ 2 1/3 cups plain (all purpose) flour

A large pinch of flaked sea salt

75g/ 2.5 oz / ½ cup shelled pistachios, roughly chopped, plus extra for decoration

200g / 7 oz / 1 cup 70 % dark chocolate or chocolate chips

METHOD FOR SHORTBREAD:
To make the shortbread place the butter, sugar and lemon zest into a large bowl and using an electric mixer beat together for about 5 minutes or until light and fluffy. Scrape the bowl down and add the flour, salt and pistachios, mixing together briefly until it comes together as a dough. Tip the dough out onto the work surface and bring together into a ball and divide into two equal pieces. Place each piece of dough between sheets of clingfilm or parchment paper and rollout into 1cm thick rectangles, about 10 inches long, wrap in clingfilm and refrigerate until firm.

Preheat the oven to 170C (150C fan)/ 340 F and line two baking trays with parchment paper. Cut the dough into 1-inch thick fingers and prick with a fork. Place the biscuits onto the prepared baking trays and bake in the preheated oven for 25-30 minutes or until lightly browned. Remove from the oven and allow to cool fully.

METHOD FOR CHOCOLATE COATING:
For the chocolate place into a heatproof bowl and microwave in 30 second bursts until about three quarters of the chocolate has melted, remove the bowl and mix vigorously with a spatula until fully melted. Dip the shortbread halfway into the chocolate, allow the excess to drip off then set onto a clean sheet of parchment, decorating with a few extra chopped pistachios. Once the chocolate has set, devour! (If you really have to, the biscuits will keep for 3-4 days in a sealed container.)

Paul's tip:

Use unrefined light muscovado sugar for a caramelly biscuit and throw in chopped white chocolate. YUM

Granny Boyd's Biscuits

Nigella Lawson

Makes: 24 biscuits

Preparation time: 30 minutes

Chilling time: 15-20 minutes

You will need: 2-3 flat baking sheets

300g self-raising flour

30g cocoa powder

250g unsalted butter (room temperature)

125g caster sugar

Preheat the oven to 170 degrees C/Gas Mark 3

Sieve flour and cocoa Powder and set it aside.

Cream butter and sugar till light and pale in color.

Mix in flour mixture, it might look like it needs liquid, but keep working the ingredients in and it will form a dough.

Roll into walnut-sized balls and arrange these on the baking sheets.

Flatten these balls with the back of the fork.

Bake for 5mins at 170 degrees C and then turn the temperature down to 150 degrees C for a further 10-15mins.

The biscuits should feel firm on top although not hard. Remove from the oven and transfer to cool on wire rack, before storing in air-tight container.

Paul's tip:

I love these biscuits but dip them in chocolate to add a touch of luxury.

Warm buckwheat waffles with gianduja, toasted chestnuts, Chantilly cream and shaved black truffle

Ollie Dabbous
Michelin starred English chef, restaurateur

Serves: 8-10

Preparation time: Start the day before, for the Chantilly cream, after that 1-2 hours

Cooking time: 1 hour depending on level of skill

You will need: A greased waffle iron, a chinois (conical metal strainer), a handblender

---

INGREDIENTS FOR THE WAFFLES:

200g Plain flour

125g Buckwheat flour

5g Salt

20g Sugar

4 medium eggs

500g Milk

1tsp Molasses

150g Butter, melted

Mix the dry ingredients together.

Blend the eggs, milk and molasses, then pass through a chinois (conical strainer) and whisk into the dry ingredients.

Whisk in the butter to the mix. Beat until smooth, but no longer than necessary. Leave in the fridge until required.

INGREDIENTS FOR THE GIANDUJA SAUCE:

250g Gianduja chocolate

175g Dark chocolate 70% cocoa

250g Whipping cream

200g Milk

35g Butter, salted

20g Caster sugar

Pinch Salt

Melt the chocolate and gianduja.

Heat the milk with the butter, sugar and salt to melt, then add to the cream, just to bring to about body temp.

Pour onto the melted chocolate, mixing well to form a smooth homogenous sauce.

INGREDIENTS FOR THE CHESTNUT PUREE:

250g Cooked vacuum packed chestnuts

400g Milk

2g Salt

60g Muscovado sugar

Place everything in a pan, bring to a boil and simmer for 5 mins.

Blend all together with a handblender and pass through a chinois.

Paul's tip:
this is THE dinner party dessert so take your time, make the components in advance and feel free to swap and change some of the ingredients like chestnuts if you can't get hold of them.

Double Chocolate & Hazelnut Brioches

Kimberley Wilson
Finalist Great British Bakeoff 2013, TV presenter, psychologist

Makes: 12 brioches

Preparation time: Start the day before

Cooking time: 16-20 minutes

You will need: A Magimix/KitchenAid with a dough hook, 12 brioche cases

---

150g good quality milk chocolate

75ml whole milk

470g strong white bread flour

30g cocoa powder

½ tsp mixed spice

7g fast action dried yeast

50g caster sugar

6 large eggs

1tsp orange blossom water (I used Nielson-Massey)

½ tsp vanilla bean paste

Zest 1 unwaxed orange

Pinch of salt

200g unsalted butter, very soft (plus extra for brushing)

50ml flavourless oil

100g chopped hazelnuts

Paul's tip:

Take two slices and sandwich lots of grated dark chocolate between and toast.... speechless enjoyment.

THE NIGHT BEFORE

In a bain marie melt the dark chocolate and milk together. Set aside to cool slightly.

In a measuring jug beat the eggs with the orange blossom water, salt, vanilla and zest.

Sift the flour, cocoa and mixed spice in to the bowl of a stand mixer fitted with a dough hook. Stir in the sugar and yeast. Start the mixer on a low speed and add the egg mixture slowly but steadily until incorporated into a sticky dough. Add the melted chocolate and butter, increase the speed and knead for 8-10 minutes.

Cover the bowl with cling film and refrigerate overnight.

THE NEXT DAY

Pre-heat oven to 200C/180C fan/gas 6.

Brush 12 brioche moulds with melted butter.

Tip the dough on to a surface dusted with cocoa powder. Divide in to 12 pieces. Pinch off roughly 1/3 of each ball of dough, so you have 12 large pieces and 12 small pieces. Roll all in to balls. Drop the 12 large balls in to the prepared moulds.

Roll the smaller balls in to the chopped hazelnuts. Dip your finger in a little cocoa powder and make a small indent in each of the larger buns. Gently press a small bun in to the top of each larger one. Cover with oiled cling film and leave in a warm place to rise for 45 minutes or until almost doubled in size.

Bake for 16-20 minutes. Serve warm with butter and good marmalade, or go for it with chocolate spread!

Strawberry Chocolate Muffins

Natasha Corrett
Health food and cookery writer

Serves: 6

Preparation time: 30 minutes

Cooking time: 25 minutes

You will need: 1 x 6 muffin tray case

200g almond flour

1 tsp baking powder

½ tsp pink salt

2 organic eggs

125ml rice milk (or plant milk of your choice)

50g raw cacao powder

1 tbsp vanilla extract

200ml coconut blossom syrup (or syrup of your choice)

100g chopped dates

8 fresh strawberries

Paul's tip:

For special occasions dip the tops of the muffins into melted dark chocolate and sit a whole strawberry on top and once set, dust with cocoa and icing sugar.

Pre-heat oven to 180 C Fan/Gas mark 4.

Separate the egg yolks and white. Put the egg whites into a bowl and whisk till they become stiff peaks.

Weigh out the almond flour, baking powder, salt and cacao powder and mix together into a second bowl.

In a third bowl mix the egg yolks, coconut blossom syrup and vanilla extract.

With a wooden spoon, mix together the dried mixture into the egg yolk mixture until combined. Fold in the egg whites with a silver spoon. Then add the chopped dates.

Pour the mixture evenly into 6 muffin tray cases.

Chop off the green tops of the strawberries and put one strawberry into the center of each muffin making sure that the filling goes over the top of the strawberry so you can't see it. (You might like to leave a little of the filling to put over the top at the end). Make sure that you fill the muffin cases right to the top.

Slice the last 2 strawberries and place them on the top of the mixture in the muffin cases to decorate.

Put into the oven for 25 minutes.

Take out the oven and leave to cool on a cooling rack.

Puddings
& Desserts

Chocolate is comfort, chocolate is luxurious, chocolate is a treat well deserved for any occasion. Chocolate is something we all look forward to. We treat ourselves to shop bought chocolate desserts and puddings to either pimp up our dinner parties or for something I believe in more than anything else - soul food. The food that you crave to feed your soul, to feed the family and to deliver a whole lot of food love. The balance of recipes in this chapter will help you whip up a dessert in minutes for a midweek dinner or impress for a weekend dinner party. Be creative, use all of the recipes as a base and let your imagination give you confidence to try something new.

Chocolate Brownie Pudding with Salted Caramel and Toffee Pecans

Emma Thompson
Actress and writer

Serves: 4

Preparation time: 45 minutes

Cooking time: 25-30 minutes

You will need: 4 individual pudding basins, or 6" baking dish

Paul's tip:

For a boozy pudding add a shot of whisky, rum or cognac to the caramel sauce.
Make in advance and freeze wrapped well in aluminium then bake from frozen for 30 minutes at 170 ° C/330° F as a fantastic last minute dessert.

100g/3.5oz/½ cup unsalted (sweet) butter

250g/8.8oz/1¼ cups unrefined caster sugar

75g /1.7 fl oz Golden Syrup (you can substitute Light Corn Syrup)

275g/9.7oz/1 ½ cups Valrhona dark chocolate (or good quality 70% dark chocolate chips)

4 medium size free range eggs

70g/2.5oz/½ cup plain (all-purpose) flour

Melt together the butter, sugar and syrup until it bubbles.

Remove from the heat and add the chocolate and mix well.

Add the eggs and beat all until smooth, then add the flour, mixing well.

Pour into a pudding basin, deep 6" deep baking dish and bake at 175°C/350° F/ Gas Mark 3.5 for 25 to 30 minutes. It should still have a wobble when it leaves the oven. Don't leave it in the oven for any longer than the listed time so that the brownie middle is still soft and molten.

SALTED CARAMEL SAUCE:

100g/3.5oz/½ cup salted butter

100g/3.5oz/½ cup unrefined light muscovado sugar

100g/3.5oz/½ cup double (heavy) cream

1 teaspoon Maldon (flaked) sea salt

To make the caramel – bring the butter and sugar to a simmer with the salt and cook for 3 minutes.

Take off the heat, add the cream and mix well.

While this is warm pour it over the brownie pudding and leave to stand.

HONEY TOFFEE PECANS:

1 tbsp honey

1 tbsp unrefined caster sugar

½ teaspoon Maldon (flaked) sea salt

100g/3.5oz/¾ cup shelled pecan nuts

On a flat baking tray, cook the pecans in the oven at 170 degrees/330 degreees F/Gas Mark 3 for 5 minutes or until golden brown.

In a saucepan bring the honey, sugar and sea salt to a simmer until golden.

Throw in the pecans and stir to coat in the caramel.

Pour on to a parchment paper and allow to cool.

Once cold, chop and break into even pieces.

Sprinkle over the pudding and serve.

Caramelised White Chocolate Mousse

Marcus Wareing
Michelin starred English chef, restaurateur

Serves: 6

Preparation time: 1 hour

Chilling time: Overnight, so start the day before

You will need: silicon baking sheet, 6 x 8.5cm individual pudding moulds

---

VANILLA CRÈME ANGLAISE:

8.5 fl oz/1 cup whole milk

8.8 fl oz/1 cup whipping cream

2 x vanilla pods, split and scraped

120g or 8 medium sized egg yolks

75g/2.5 oz/1/4 cup caster sugar

1 tbsp Trimoline (liquid invert sugar) or liquid clear honey

THE MOUSSE:

350g/12 fl oz Vanilla Crème Anglaise, as above

660g/ 3 ½ cups white chocolate, or white chocolate chips, caramelized (see method on p138)

2 leaves gelatin soaked in cold water until soft.

600g/20 fl oz/2 ½ cups whipping cream, softly whipped

Bring the milk, cream and vanilla to the boil.

Whisk the yolks and sugar together and combine gently with the cream. Pour back into the pan and simmer slowly until it thickens to coat the back of a spoon.

Take the pan off the heat and whisk in the Trimoline or liquid honey. Pass through a fine sieve into a bowl and put straight into the fridge to chill quickly.

For the caramelized chocolate, lay the white chocolate/chocolate chips on a silicon baking sheet and bake in the oven at 170°c turning every 15 minutes until uniformly caramelized.

Warm the Creme Anglaise and dissolve the gelatin in to it,

Pour over the chocolate and whisk well.

Pass through a sieve or fine strainer.

Ensuring the chocolate mix is not hot,gently fold in the whipped cream.

Pour into the moulds and freeze.

To serve, defrost in the fridge over night.

Paul's tip:
For a dinner party showstopper, sprinkle the top of each mousse while still frozen and use a blowtorch to caramelize for a crunchy and golden finish.

Chocolate and Avocado Mousse

Brian Blessed
OBE, actor

Serves: 6

Preparation time: 5 minutes

Cooking time: 10 minutes

Chilling time: 3 hours at least

100g (3 ½ oz) dark chocolate

4 tbsp maple syrup

2 tsp vanilla bean paste or extract

5 tbsp almond milk or coconut milk drink

2 ½ tbsp cocoa, sieved

2 large ripe avocados, flesh scooped out

Set aside 25g (1oz) chocolate for decoration and break the rest into squares. Melt in a heatproof bowl set over a pan of shallow, simmering water. Stir in the maple syrup, vanilla, almond or coconut milk, ¼ tsp fine salt and the cocoa until smooth.

In a blender or food processor, whizz the chocolate mixture with the avocado flesh until silky smooth. Divide the mixture between 6 small serving glasses. Chill for at least 3 hours, or for up to 12 hours.

To make the decoration, scrape the edge of the reserved chocolate using a vegetable peeler to make long shards. Store in an airtight container until needed. Scatter over the mousse just before serving.

Paul's tip:

Drizzle a little fruity olive oil over for a very sophisticated dessert.

Easy Rich Chocolate Mousse

Darcey Bussell
CBE, ballerina, TV presenter

Serves: 4

Preparation time: 30 minutes

Chilling time: 2-3 hours

You will need: 4 x pudding ramekins

225g plain dark 70% chocolate, broken into small pieces

4 eggs

15mls rum (excluded for children, Mum and Dad can have it!)

15g butter

Separate the eggs, making sure the egg whites are in a large bowl.

Melt the chocolate in a heatproof bowl over a saucepan of simmering water. Stir in egg yolks one at a time, then the butter, until all are dissolved.

Whisk the egg whites in a clean dry bowl until stiff and then fold them into chocolate mixture.

Pour into 4 small dishes and put into fridge for 2-3 hours

Chocolate Pots
with Tejas de Tolosa Biscuits

José Pizarro
Critically acclaimed Spanish chef, restaurateur

Serves: 6-8

Preparation time: 30 minutes for biscuits, 20 minutes for the chocolate pots

Cooking time: 6-8 minutes for biscuits

Chilling time: 3 hours at least for chocolate pots

You will need: 2 flat baking sheets lined with baking paper, 6 ramekins

---

INGREDIENTS FOR THE CHOCOLATE POTS:

200g dark 70% chocolate broken into pieces

75ml full-fat (whole) milk, warmed to blood temperature

200ml double cream, taken from the fridge 20 minutes before using

INGREDIENTS FOR THE TEJAS DE TOLOSA BISCUITS:

1 free range egg white

50g caster sugar

1 tbsp plain flour

A few drops vanilla extract

25g unsalted butter, melted and cooled

Flaked almonds to sprinkle

Preheat the oven to 190°C. Line two baking sheets with baking paper.

To make the biscuits, beat the egg white and caster sugar with a fork until frothy. Sift over the flour and fold in. Add the vanilla extract, then lastly add the cooled melted butter.

Spoon the mixture onto the baking sheets in dollops about 8 cm wide. Sprinkle with the flaked almonds, if using, and bake for 6–8 minutes until lightly golden.

Have a rolling pin ready and, as soon as the biscuits are out of the oven, lay them over the rolling pin so that they cool and harden in a curled shape. Set aside on a wire rack.

Melt the chocolate in a bain-marie until smooth. Very slowly add the milk, then the cream. Pour into six small pots or glasses and leave to set in a cool place (or in the fridge if your kitchen is very hot) before serving with the biscuits.

Paul's tip:

Great made in advance for picnics and midnight snacks.

Chocolate Tart with Crème Fraiche

Rowley Leigh
Critically acclaimed English chef, restaurateur

Serves: 6-8

Preparation time: 1 hour

Cooking time: 20 mins for tart case, 20 minutes for filling

You will need: 26mm loose bottomed tart tin

INGREDIENTS FOR THE FILLING:

300g bitter chocolate

4 egg yolks

2 eggs

60g caster sugar

Crème fraiche, to serve

INGREDIENTS FOR THE PASTRY:

65g butter

50g caster sugar

1 egg, beaten

125g plain flour

Paul's tip:

If you prefer a deeper tart then simply use a smaller taller tart ring for this classic recipe.

Preheat the oven to 180 C/ Gas mark 4.

It is important not to overcook the chocolate mixture or it will dry up rather alarmingly. If it is still a bit runny, there will be absolutely no harm done.

For the pastry, cream the butter and sugar together in a food mixer or in a bowl with a wooden spoon. When they are perfectly smooth, mix in the beaten egg to form a wet paste. Sift in the flour with a pinch of salt and fold it in very gently without working the dough. Collect together in a ball, wrap in clingfilm and refrigerate for at least an hour.

Butter a 26cm loose-bottomed tart tin. Roll out the dough to fit the tin and, collecting it on the rolling pin, drop it into the tin. Push the dough well into the corners, ensuring there is a 1cm overlap all round the edge. Trim off any excess. Cover with clingfilm and chill for one hour, then line with greaseproof paper, fill with baking beans and bake in an oven preheated to 180 degree / Gas Mark 4 for twenty minutes. Remove the beans and cook the pastry for another five minute , until just starting to colour.

Melt the chocolate, either in a bowl set over a pan of simmering water or in a microwave. Whisk the egg yolks, eggs and sugar together until they form a thick, white, frothy cream. Pour in the chocolate and blend to a rich, dark cream. Pour this mixture into the tart case, return to the oven and bake for twelve to fifteen minutes, by which time the mixture should be just set. This tart is best served lukewarm, with the crème fraiche or a little cream or icecream.

Chocolate Tart

Marco Pierre White
Michelin starred English chef, restaurateur

Serves: 10

Preparation time: 1 hour

Cooking time: 45 minutes

You will need: 1 x 20cm sweet pastry lined tart ring baked blind

---

INGREDIENTS FOR THE SWEET PASTRY:

500 g plain flour

175 g icing sugar

250 g unsalted butter, at room temperature

1 vanilla pod, split open

1½ eggs, beaten

INGREDIENTS FOR THE CHOCOLATE FILLING:

500g Valrhona Equatorial dark chocolate, broken into pieces.

3 eggs

200mls milk

350mls double cream

TO SERVE:

Chocolate shavings (use a potato peeler or cheese slice)

Icing sugar

Paul's tip:

This is a classic not to be messed with but my top tip is always serve it at room temperature.

Sift the flour and icing sugar on to a work surface and work in the butter. Make a well in the centre and add the seeds scraped from the vanilla pod. Add the eggs. Knead the mixture with your fingers, working as quickly as you can, until everything is combined to a smooth dough. Wrap in plastic film and leave to rest in the fridge for at least 30 minutes.

Pre-heat the oven to 180°C/350

Grease a flan tin with a removable base that is 20 cm in diameter and 3.75 cm deep. Roll out the pastry on a lightly floured surface to a disc large enough to line the tin and allowing an overhang of not less than 1 cm. Lay the pastry gently into the tin.

Line the pastry case with greaseproof paper and fill with enough dry baking beans or lentils (or indeed any dry pulses) to insure the sides as well as the bottom are weighted. Bake for 10 minutes. Remove the beans and greaseproof paper and trim off the overhanging pastry, then return the flan case to the oven to bake for a further 10 minutes.

Meanwhile, make the chocolate filling. Melt the chocolate in a bowl over a bain-marie (or a bowl over a saucepan of simmering water), this should not be too warm.

Whisk the eggs together in a large bowl

Bring the milk and cream to the boil in a pan, then pour onto the eggs and whisk together.

Pass through a sieve on to the chocolate and mix well. Pour this into the blind-baked tart case.

Put the tart into the oven, and immediately turn the oven off, Leave the tart in the oven for 40 to 45 minutes.

When cool, trim the edges of the pastry and cut the tart into 10 portions. Serve with chocolate shavings on the top, and sprinkled with icing sugar.

Mocha Tart

Roger Pizey
Critically acclaimed English chef, author, TV Presenter

Serves: 8

Preparation time: 30 minutes for pastry/20 minutes for filling

Cooking time: 1 hour for pastry/1 hour for filling

You will need: 26mm x 15mm tart ring with removable base

INGREDIENTS FOR THE SWEET PASTRY:

112g Butter

42g icing sugar

1 egg yolk

10 ml water

150g plain flour, sifted

INGREDIENTS FOR THE FILLING:

525ml double cream

340g dark (70%) chocolate

30ml coffee essence

340g milk chocolate

Cream the butter and sugar together. Then add the egg yolk and half the water and mix.
Mix in the sifted flour slowly, then add the rest of the water.

Knead slowly on a cool, floured work surface.

Wrap the dough in clingfilm and allow to rest in the fridge, preferably overnight,or for at least 2 hours. Remove from the fridge 30 minutes before you need it.

Preheat the oven to 180 C/Gas mark 4. Roll out the dough on a floured surface and line a 260mm x 15mm tart ring with it. Leave in the fridge for an hour and then blind bake for 15-20 minutes until golden brown.

Bring 275ml of the double cream to a simmer. Leave for 2 minutes and pour over the dark chocolate. Mix until fully melted. Pour into the cooked and cooled tart base and leave to set in the fridge for at least 30 minutes.

Pour the coffee essence into the rest of the double cream and bring to a simmer. Leave for 2 minutes and pour over the milk chocolate. Mix until fully melted. Pour into tart and leave to set in a cool place (not the fridge as will set too hard)

Decorate with dark and white chocolate shavings.

Delicious with salted caramel or coffee ice cream!

Paul's tip:

Use different varieties of cold espresso for a new flavour dimension instead of coffee essence .

Rose and Dark Chocolate Ice Cream

Eimear Cook

Serves: 6-8

Preparation time: 30 minutes plus churning time

Chilling time: 30 minutes before churning

You will need: An ice cream maker

INGREDIENTS FOR THE CUSTARD:

500 mls double cream

300 mls milk

200mls rose water

250g caster sugar

12 egg yolks

100g dark chocolate chopped into small pieces.

Dried rose petals to garnish

Bring the milk, cream, and rose water to the simmer.

Whisk the egg yolks and sugar together until smooth.

Pour the simmering liquid onto the egg mixture and whisk well.

Add the chocolate and whisk until melted in fully

Immediately cling film and leave until fully cold.

Mix well and churn in an ice cream machine.

INGREDIENTS FOR THE SYRUP:

200mls rose water

200g caster sugar

For the syrup, put the ingredients in a saucepan, bring to a simmer and cool.

TO SERVE:

Freeze a glass or ice cream coupe

Scoop a generous sized ball of ice cream by dipping the scoop into hot water first.

Place in the centre of the frozen coupe.

Spoon over two tablespoons of syrup.

Sprinkle over edible dried rose petals.

Paul's tip:

Try having a rose float, with cloudy lemonade and a scoop of this fragrant ice cream.

Chocolate and Salted Caramel Cheesecake

Glenn Cosby
Finalist Great British Bakeoff 2013

Serves: 8-10

Preparation time: 1 hour , plus chill overnight

Cooking time: 10 minutes for base/25 minutes for filling

You will need: a 23cm cake tin with removable base, lined with baking paper

---

Ingredients for the base:

200g biscuit Oreo biscuit crumbs (you only want the biscuits so buy two packs)

1 tablespoon caster sugar

30g salted butter, melted

Ingredients for the filling:

500g full fat cream cheese

100g caster sugar

150g/ml double cream

4 eggs

300g dark 70% chocolate, melted (I recommend Willie's Cacao Chef Drops)

Ingredients for the salted caramel:

200g caster sugar

150g double cream

1 teaspoon of sea salt flakes

Paul's tip:

This is a full on decadent dessert so a cheeky spoon of very cold Greek yoghurt will help balance the sweetness.

Preheat an oven to 180°C/160°C fan/gas mark 4. The line a loose-based 23cm (9 inch) cake tin with greaseproof paper.

You'll need to start with the tedious business of scraping off the cream between the biscuits; sorry about that. Then blitz them in a Magimix and mix with the sugar before pouring in the melted butter and stirring. Tip the mixture into the cake tin and spread around to cover the base of the tin. I like to push some up the sides too but that's up to you. Don't press too hard though.

Bake the base for 10 minutes and then allow to cool.

Place the cream cheese, sugar and cream in a mixer bowl and mix until it is well combined, then add the eggs one at a time. You don't want to whip it though - use a mixer with a paddle attachment or a spatula, then pour in the melted chocolate and mix to combine.

Pour the filling onto the cooked base, and bake for about 25 minutes. Remove from the oven and allow to rest and cool completely. Ideally it should rest in the fridge overnight.

If you're not resting it overnight, then while it bakes, make the caramel. In a medium saucepan melt 150g of caster sugar over a gentle heat watching constantly.

Don't use a wooden spoon or anything else in the caramel or it will stick to the utensil so to help it melt by gently swirling the pan so that the melted sugar mixes with the solid sugar.

Once the sugar has all melted into a golden caramel carefully pour in the double cream - be careful as this will splutter and give off a lot of steam. You can now use a wooden spoon or a spatula and stir it over a low heat until it goes from a sticky mess to a smooth caramel sauce.

Add the salt and allow the caramel sauce to cool.

When you are ready to serve the cheesecake take it carefully out of the tin and peel off the greaseproof power. At the last minute pour the salted caramel over the top and watch it run.

Chocolate Orange Cheesecake

Anna Pancaldi
Singer, songwriter

Serves: 8

Preparation time: 40 minutes

Chilling time: 1 hour

You will need: a metal tart tin with removable base

INGREDIENTS FOR THE BASE:

16 HobNobs (or digestives or graham crackers)

120 g unsalted butter

INGREDIENTS FOR THE FILLING:

200 g Philadelphia cream cheese

185ml double cream

100g icing sugar

250g Terry's Chocolate Orange (or orange flavoured chocolate)

Paul's tip:

Try covering the top of this delicious cheese cake with marmalade for extra zing.

Crush the HobNobs in a bowl with the end of a rolling pin until they are of a breadcrumb consistency.

Melt the butter in a saucepan, add the crushed breadcrumbs and mix thoroughly. Add the biscuit mix to the tart tin, press down firmly, evenly covering the base, and put in the fridge to cool for around 30-40 minutes.

In another bowl mix together the cream cheese (Philadelphia) and icing sugar.

In a separate bowl whisk together the cream until stiff peaks are formed.

Melt 160g of chocolate orange in glass bowl over barely simmering water on a pan making sure the water doesn't touch the bottom of the bowl.

Once melted, stir the melted chocolate into the whipped cream and then add this to the cream cheese mixture and whisk for a minute or two.

Pour the mixture onto the cooled biscuit base and put back in the fridge for 20 minutes or so.

To decorate, grate some chocolate on top with edible pansies to add some colour.

Cacao Twin Peaks

Willie Harcourt-Cooze
Chocolatier, TV presenter

Serves: 6

Preparation time: 45 minutes

Chilling time: 1 hour or more

You will need: 7 cm diameter dome shaped silicone moulds or ramekins

INGREDIENTS FOR THE MOUSSE:

6 eggs separated *

300g Willie's Cacao Peruvian Chulucanas 70% dark chocolate. Its soft fruity notes pair perfectly with the coulis

80g raw cane sugar

450ml lightly whipped double cream *

* both the eggs and the cream are best used at room temperature

INGREDIENTS FOR THE COULIS:

250g raspberries blitzed and sieved

INGREDIENTS FOR THE CHOCOLATE CASES:

50g Willie's Cacao Peruvian Chulucanas 70% dark chocolate

Paul's tip:

Practice your tempering before making this dessert so your chocolate domes are shiny and smooth.

TO PREPARE THE CHOCOLATE CASES

Melt the dark chocolate in a bowl over simmering water taking care the water does not touch the bottom of the bowl and stirring constantly and brush the melted chocolate onto the inside of the silicone moulds. Put in the fridge until set and hard.

TO PREPARE THE MOUSSE

Beat the egg yolks with ½ the sugar until creamy white.

Beat the egg whites with the other ½ of the sugar until they form soft peaks.

Melt the dark chocolate in a bowl over simmering water taking care the water does not touch the bottom of the bowl and stirring constantly

Lightly whip the cream until it just holds its shape

Combine a couple of table spoons of lightly whipped cream with the egg yolk mixture, then add the chocolate and then the rest of the lightly whipped cream.

Fold in the softly peaked beaten egg whites

TO ASSEMBLE AND SERVE

Spoon or pipe the mousse into the chocolate cases or ramekins

Pipe raspberry coulis into the centre of each mousse

If you are turning out the mousses, keep them in the fridge for an hour first or until set.

Serve with fresh raspberries on the side for decoration

Quick Chocolate Pear Crumbles

Fay Ripley
Actress, cookery writer

Serves: 4

Preparation time: 5 minutes

Cooking time: 20 minutes

You will need: A small ovenproof dish

20g blanched hazelnuts

3 dark chocolate digestives

2 big ripe pears (they must be ripe or this won't work)

30g dark 70% chocolate roughly broken up

Preheat the oven to 180C (fan)/200 C/gas mark 6.

In a plastic food bag, bash the nuts and biscuits to break them up into rough crumbs.

Cut the pears in half and scoop out the core with a teaspoon. Place the pears in a small ovenproof dish and fill with the crumbs.

Bake for 20 minutes, then for a final 5 minutes add the chocolate pieces (they burn quite easily if cooked for longer than this).

When the chocolate has melted, remove from the oven and serve with a ball of vanilla ice cream on top.

Paul's tip:

Take care not to burn the chocolate when baking so check a few times while cooking.

Chocolate and Raspberry Pudding Cake with Chocolate Ganache

Tamasin Day-Lewis
Cookery writer

Serves: 8-10

Preparation time: 40 minutes

Cooking time: 45 minutes

INGREDIENTS FOR THE CAKE:

4 organic eggs, separated, plus one whole egg

175g/6oz vanilla caster sugar

225g/8oz best bitter chocolate, minimum

70% cocoa solids, I use Green and Black

150g/5oz blanched almonds, freshly ground

1 heaped tsp ground coffee

200g/7oz fresh raspberries

INGREDIENTS FOR THE GANACHE:

225g/8oz dark chocolate

125ml/4fl oz double cream

Preheat oven to 170°C/325°F/Gas 3

Whisk the egg yolks and egg together with half the sugar, until pale and doubled in volume.

Melt the chocolate in a double saucepan.

Whisk the egg whites, adding the sugar a bit at a time, until they are at the satiny, soft peak stage. Add half of them to the egg and sugar mixture, folding them in gently. Add the chocolate and the rest of the whites, folding as you go. Then do likewise with the almonds and coffee. Last of all, add the raspberries, which need folding in with extreme gentleness so that they don't break up.

Scrape the mixture into a greased and floured 20cm/8in Springform tin, with a circle of greased greaseproof paper laid on its base, and bake for 30 minutes. Then turn the oven off and leave the cake in for another 15 minutes or until a skewer comes out clean from the centre. Remove from the oven and leave to cool in the tin.

Scald the cream in a small pan, remove from the heat and stir in the broken up chocolate.

Cover the cake with the ganache and leave to cool.

Paul's tip:

Works incredibly well with mixed berries and a touch of mint and basil.

Chocolate and Chestnut Marquise

Tamasin Day-Lewis
Cookery writer

Serves: 10

Preparation time: 45 minutes

Chilling time: 24 hours

3 x 200g/7oz packs of vacuum-packed chestnuts, the best you can find

125g/4oz unsalted butter, melted in a pan

125g/4oz unrefined vanilla sugar

200g/7oz best bitter chocolate, minimum

70% cocoa solids

1 tbsp Cognac

1 tbsp water

4 organic eggs, separated

Put the chestnuts in a food processor with the melted butter and all but a tablespoon of the sugar. Blend until well mixed. Melt the chocolate in a double boiler with the brandy and water, add it to the chestnut mixture and blitz briefly. Stir in the egg yolks one by one, then whisk the egg whites to soft peak stage. Add the remaining tablespoon of sugar and whisk until stiff. Stir the first tablespoon into the chestnut mixture, then fold in the rest as well as you can; the mixture will be very thick and sludgy at this stage. Plop it into a loaf tin, which you have greased lightly with an unobtrusive oil such as almond oil, and smooth down the surface. Leave to cool and put it in the fridge when cold.

I think this is best eaten after a day or two, so you can make it in advance. It will turn out beautifully on to a flat dish. Serve with pouring cream, to which you can add a tablespoon of freshly made coffee if you like. A couple of slices each are all you will want. The other route would be to serve it with a whipped, sugared crème chantilly. Killer.

Paul's tip:

I pour Baileys over this for a festive dessert to challenge even the best Christmas pudding.

Savoury Chocolate

Using chocolate in savoury recipes may sound a little unusual and daunting at first. I have quite strong opinions about drowning great meats like venison in bitter chocolate sauce…it's outdated and a bit old fashioned. Think aromatic, rich and fragrant flavours. Chocolate has so much texture and life, and when it's used carefully will add a flavour dimension and richness of colour to many every day foods, including a simple steak. It's not always about melted chocolate - there's cocoa powder and coco nibs with crunch and a flavour that will fill your head with aromatic depth and richness….read on to be inspired. Did I mention the toasted cheese and chocolate sandwich?

Fillet of Beef with Crushed Black Pepper and Red Chilli in a Dark Chocolate Infused Port Wine and Balvenie Whisky Sauce

Cyrus Todiwala OBE
Chef and restauranteur

Paul's tip:

If you can't find Balvenie Caribbean Cask 14 Yrs. Old then use your favourite whisky, but for a balanced flavour don't go for heavy peated varieties.

Serves: 4

Preparation time: 30 minutes

Cooking time: 20 minutes

You will need: a frying or griddle pan.

1kg/2.2lb beef fillet, the finest quality you can find

FOR THE MARINADE

1 heaped tbsp crushed hot red chilli

1 tbsp crushed black peppercorns

1 tbsp finely crushed fresh ginger

1 tbsp finely crushed peeled garlic

1 tsp ground cumin

2 tsps ground coriander

2 tbsp tamarind pulp

1 tsp crushed sea salt

2 tbsps groundnut or vegetable oil

FOR THE SAUCE:

(For our sauce we use Cru Virrunga 70% dark chocolate buttons, but use any dark unsweetened chocolate of good quality). Whisky used was Balvenie Caribbean Cask 14 Yrs. Old

2 tbsp unsalted butter

100g/3.5 oz/ ½ cup dark chocolate or chocolate chips

150 ml/5 fl oz port wine

500 ml/17 fl oz beef stock

2 banana or ratte shallots, finely chopped

2 tsps balsamic vinegar

Combine all of the above in a large bowl and mix together thoroughly to make a paste. Add the fillet to the bowl and smear the paste all over the beef covering it completely.

Cover with clingfilm and refrigerate for at least three to four hours.

Preheat the oven to 220*C/428 F/ Gas Mark 7 and keep a wire rack in your oven tray ready.

On the hob, heat a large non-stick frying that can fit the fillet of beef.

When hot but not sizzling, add the marinated beef fillet.

Fry for a minute or two on the same side and gradually turn the fillet over, so that all the sides have been well browned - about 1 minute on each side.

Switch off the hob, and put the frying pan to one side. Lift the beef and place it on the rack and into the oven on the top shelf, for about fifteen minutes.

Meanwhile add the butter to the pan, which will have cooled slightly, and return the pan to a medium heat.

When the butter melts add the finely chopped shallots and when pale and soft add the stock and let the mixture come to the boil.

Reduce the stock by gently boiling for a few minutes, then add the balsamic vinegar, the whisky and the port wine.

Reduce the liquid further by a third, ensuring that any whisky has burned off, then whisk in the chocolate pieces until melted and well blended.

Bring back to a simmer and taste.

Add salt & pepper to taste.

Remove the beef from the oven and let it rest for a few minutes before you carve and serve with the sauce. Resting your beef is essential as it allows the fibres and proteins to relax before eating.

Chocolate ketchup

Paul A Young

Makes: 4 x 350mls jars or bottles

Preparation time: 15 minutes

Cooking time: 40 minutes

You will need: 4 jars or bottles, sterilized
(see p141 for sterilizing method)

---

2 red onions

2 cloves of garlic

250mls/8 fl oz /1 cup Cider
Vinegar

750mls / 25 fl oz / 3 cups Passatta

1 tbsp tomato puree

2 tbsp fresh thyme leaves

100g/3 oz / ¾ cup light
muscovado sugar

50g/ 1.8 oz / ⅓ cup milk chocolate
or chocolate chips

75g / 2.6 oz / ½ cup dark
chocolate or chocolate chips

1 tsp 5 spice powder

1 tsp Maldon or cracked sea salt

Pinch of black pepper

1 tbsp light olive oil

Finely chop the onion and garlic and sweat in a saucepan with the olive oil until soft.

Add the salt, pepper and thyme.

Add the passatta, tomato puree, cider vinegar, sugar and five spice. Simmer very gently for 40 minutes.

Add the milk and dark chocolate and stir until melted then blend.
Fill in to sterilized bottles or jars and allow to cool, then refrigerate.

Paul's tip:

Enjoy as you would your usual ketchup but especially enjoy with bacon sandwiches and freshly cooked French fries.

For a fiery ketchup add two teaspoons of dried chipotle chilli at the start of cooking and enjoy on pulled pork or slowly cooked brisket.

Olive Tapenade with Chocolate

Chantal Coady
Master Chocolatier Rococo Chocolates

Serves: 4 as a canapé

Preparation time: 10 minutes

---

1 290g jar pitted kalamata olives -or similar. Pit your own if you can be bothered!

5/6 preserved anchovy fillets, drained and chopped

1 large clove of garlic, chopped

2 tablespoons capers, vinegar squeezed out

5 tablespoons good quality olive oil, plus more if you want to keep it

Fresh chilli to taste

2 tablespoons rum (optional)

25g good dark chocolate, melted

Put all the ingredients except the melted chocolate into the food processor, and pulse them until everything is mixed but still retains some texture.

Add the chocolate when this is done, and stir in.

Serve on toasts if you like or as a dip, or you could use it as a base, spread on pastry, for a tomato tart or pin wheel savoury pastries for drinks. I like to add fresh goat's cheese to it, on a piece of toast.

Chocolate, Cheese and Anchovies on toast

Paul A Young

Serves: 2

Preparation time: 10 minutes

Cooking time: 5 minutes

---

4 slices of good quality thick sliced white bread

20g soft salted butter

80g 70 to 75% cocoa solids dark chocolate

1 tin of anchovy fillets (salted or in oil)

150g unpasteurized or very mature cheddar cheese

25g freshly grated Parmesan

freshly ground black pepper

Pre heat your grill for 5 minutes.

Butter the bread right to the edges.

Chop the chocolate into very small pieces and cover the bread slices evenly.

Lay two anchovy fillets in a cross on to each slice.

Grate over the cheese so it spills over the edges and grind the pepper on top.

Grill until the cheese is very golden and bubbling.

Eat and enjoy my favourite brunch, snack or lunch with a huge mug of tea.

Paul's tips

Feel free to pimp it up with different cheeses or chilli and it can even be made into a toasted sandwich. It's great made from French toast for the best brunch ever.

Stilton and Dark Chocolate Butter

Paul A Young

Makes: 1 x 250g 'log' of butter

Preparation time: 30 minutes

Chilling time: 1 hour

You will need: Double layered sheets of cling film

200g soft unsalted butter

100g mature Stilton

2 tbsp cocoa powder

1 tbsp warm water

In a food mixer beat the butter until smooth on a medium speed, add the stilton crumbled in and mix for one minute.

Mix the cocoa powder and warm water together until smooth, add to the cheese and butter mixture and taste. Feel free to add salt if your taste buds need it.

Lay out a double layered sheet of cling film and scrape out the butter and roll into a log wrapping the cling film around the butter and tie at each end.

Refrigerate for at least an hour before slicing and enjoying. It can be kept in the fridge for up to a month in an air tight container.

Paul's tips

Transform all your sandwiches, steaks, and grilled meat and fish. Its rich, smooth, salty and a little unusual but melts with a beautiful chocolatey cheesy and salty taste.

Chocolate Chutney

Paul A Young

Makes: 4 x 200g jars

Preparation time: 15 minutes

Cooking time: 45 minutes

You will need: 4 x sterilized 200g jars
(see p141 for sterilizing method)

---

2 medium white onions

2 Braeburn or Cox apples peeled

2 William or Rocha pears peeled

4 cloves of garlic

3 whole dried chillies

2 tbspn olive oil

250mls white wine vinegar

1 tin chopped tomatoes

200g Billington's unrefined light muscovado sugar

½ teaspoon five spice

1 teaspoon Maldon sea salt

½ teaspoon freshly ground black pepper

100g 70% dark chocolate

Chop the onions, apples, and pears into 1cm dice and place into a medium saucepan. Crush the garlic and add along with the chillies and olive oil.

Saute until all the ingredients have softened -this will take 15 minutes.

Add the white wine vinegar, tomatoes, sugar, 5 spice, sea salt and pepper and simmer on a low heat for 45 minutes.

Take off the heat and add the chocolate, mixing until it is melted and smooth.

Fill sterilized jars and label with date so they can be enjoyed within 6 months.

Paul's tips

This rich and well balanced chutney is amazing with savoury pies and cheeses, is super easy to make and keeps for months. Experiment with different types of chocolate for a stronger or more delicate flavour.

White Chocolate, Dill and Brown Shrimps

Paul A Young

Serves: 4

Preparation time: 10 minutes

Chilling time: 15 minutes

You will need: 4 white ramekins

400g brown shrimps

75g white chocolate (it must only contain cocoa butter and not vegetable fat)

100mls fish stock – from cube or bones

1 tablespoon chopped dill

Half lemon zested

White pepper freshly ground

½ teaspoon of Maldon sea salt

splash of Pernod

Wash the shrimps and drain well.

Portion into 4 separate small pots

In a saucepan place all the ingredients and warm on a very low heat until melted and smooth.

Pour onto each pot of shrimps and allow to cool, then refrigerate for 15 minutes before eating with oatcakes or brown bread and butter.

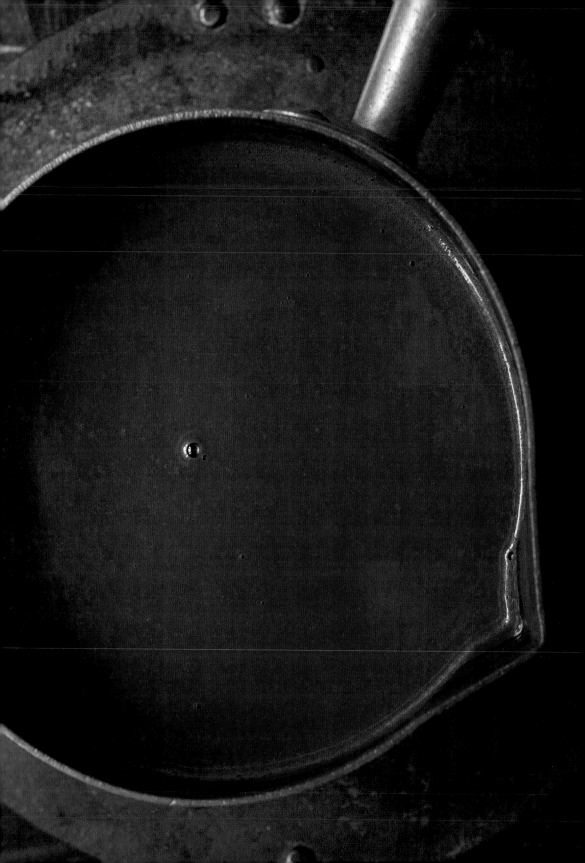

Drinks

Growing up I often enjoyed hot chocolate by mixing pure cocoa powder, sugar and milk together in the old fashioned way. This was considered quite sophisticated given the invention of instant hot chocolate, in which real chocolate was replaced with flavourings and thickeners. This chapter looks at proper hot chocolate and how to make it. Treat this recipe as your 'Hero' and let everything else follow. Hot, cold, sweet and alcoholic - chocolate can be successfully used in all these recipes. I promise you, once you have tried real chocolate in your drinks, you won't be tempted back to instant or 'chocolate flavoured' powders ever again.

Bourbon chocolate hard shake

Paul A Young

Serves: 2

Preparation time: 20 minutes

You will need: A liquid blender

500 ml/17 fl oz / 2 cups whole milk

50g/1.8 oz / 1/3 cup unrefined light muscovado sugar

100g milk chocolate or chocolate chips, melted

2 large scoops of vanilla ice cream

1 double shot of Bourbon

50g/1.8oz/ 1/3 cup dark chocolate melted

To make the milk shake warm the milk, sugar and milk chocolate just until the chocolate melts.

Allow to cool then pour into a blender.

Add the ice cream and bourbon and blend for 20 seconds.

Dip the rim of a jar or glass in the melted chocolate and fill with the frothy shake...Drink responsibly.

Hot Chocolate

Paul A Young

Serves: 4

Preparation time: 10 minutes

---

500 mls/ 17 fl oz / 2 cups water

100g/3.5 oz/ ½ cup unrefined golden caster sugar

25g / 1 oz / 1/3 cup cocoa powder

100g/3.5 oz/ ½ cup 70% dark chocolate broken into pieces or chocolate chips

In a saucepan, bring the water, sugar and cocoa powder to a simmer for 2 minutes.

Add the chocolate and whisk until the chocolate has melted.

Just before serving whisk very well until frothy, then pour into a drinking receptacle of your choice.

Paul's tips

Make in advance and store in the fridge until needed and reheat in a saucepan.

Add spices while cooking for an aromatic hot chocolate.

Add a measure of whisky or brandy for a warming winter hot chocolate

Chocolate Tea Punch

Paul A Young

Makes: 4 x 200ml cups

Preparation time: 10 minutes

You will need: A liquid blender

500mls of your favourite hot tea using 1 bag per 100mls or one teaspoon of leaves.

75g Billingtons unrefined caster sugar

100mls whole milk

100g milk chocolate melted

50mls port

50mls rum

Place all the ingredients into a blender and whizz up for a few seconds.

Serve immediately or put in a flask for a cold winter's walk.

Paul's tips

I love a good punch, they make a party really go with a swing usually due to their eye watering alcohol content and this one does have a kick but a mellow and rich finish from milky tea and chocolate. It's a great winter warmer too.

Iced Yoghurt and Salted Chocolate Smoothie

Paul A Young

Makes: 2 large glasses

Preparation time: 15 minutes

Chilling time: 15 minutes

You will need: a liquid blender

500mls whole milk

250g full fat Greek yoghurt

1 tspn Maldon sea salt

1 tbspn cocoa nibs

100g 64% Madagascan chocolate or your favourite chocolate

1 tbspn runny honey

In a saucepan, warm the honey, milk, salt chocolate and cocoa nibs together until the chocolate is fully melted.

Cool for 15 minutes.

In a blender throw in a few ice cubes, pour in the chocolate milk mixture and add the Greek yoghurt. Whizz up for 15 seconds and serve.

<u>Paul's tips</u>

Here a smoothie can be an indulgent comfort rather than a healthy option, and this recipe can be used as a summer replacement for a rich chocolatey dessert

Molten Hot Chocolate

Chris Tarrant

Serves: 4

Preparation time: 20 minutes

Cooking time: 10 minutes

INGREDIENTS FOR CHOCOLATE:

1 litre whole milk

115 ml double (heavy) cream

280g high quality 70% dark chocolate, chopped in small pieces

OPTIONS FOR FLAVOURINGS:

2 teaspoons Chinese five-spice powder

Finely grated peel of one tangerine,

75g smooth peanut butter

1 teaspoon banana extract

3 tablespoons instant coffee

75g pureed raspberries, strained and mixed with 30g caster sugar

Put the milk and cream in a heavy saucepan and bring them to a boil. Add the chocolate, reduce the heat to low, and stir until the chocolate is melted. Beat the mixture with a wire whisk until light and fluffy, 10 to 12 minutes (or use a hand blender, whipping for 5 to 6 minutes). Add the flavouring of your choice, remove from the heat and let stand for 20 minutes to allow the flavour to infuse.

If making the hot chocolate several hours in advance, transfer it to a bowl and put it in the refrigerator in a larger bowl filled with ice. When ready to serve, reheat slowly to the boiling point and whip briefly again. Serve in heatproof glasses, and top each one with whipped cream.

Chilli Hot Chocolate

Amandeep

Serves: 4

Preparation time: 15 minutes

Cooking time: 15 minutes

---

3 cups whole milk

75ml Single Cream

6tbsp whipped double cream

1 dried medium red chilli

1 cinnamon stick

25g Drinking Chocolate Powder

pinch nutmeg

150g 70 per cent good quality dark chocolate – roughly chopped

small pinch of dried chillies to garnish

Heat the milk, cinnamon, nutmeg and dry chilli in a heavy based saucepan, over a medium to high heat. Bring to the boil, leave to one side for 8-10min to infuse.

Strain through a sieve into a clean pan, and reheat on a low heat for 2-3min (don't boil).

Lower the heat, add the chocolate powder and pieces, whisk continuously until smooth and melted.

Serve with whipped cream and chocolate grating – an optional choice would be for a very small sprinkle of chilli flakes over the top, for an extra kick.

Off Piste Hot Chocolate

Cleo Rocos

Serves: 1

Preparation time: 15 minutes

Cooking time: 5 minutes

High quality dark chocolate cocoa powder

35 mls AquaRiva Reposado Tequila

15 mls AquaRiva Organic Agave Syrup

1 dash of cayenne powder

1 dash of sea salt

1 small carton whipping cream for topping

Prepare hot chocolate according to directions on the label. In a mug, stir together 100 mls of hot chocolate, tequila, agave syrup, cayenne and salt and top with fresh whipped cream.

Truffles, Gifts and Treats

Giving gifts is great, giving gifts you have made is amazing, and it's one of the reasons I own a chocolate business as it gives so much pleasure to so many including myself.... Making chocolates and chocolate gifts can be complicated in places and you may need a little practice with some of the techniques, but persevere and your efforts will be rewarded. Simple hand rolled truffles will always elicit a 'wow' and a smile from the recipient. Don't try to be too perfect but do try to be very creative especially with flavours and decorations.

Treats should be just that, little mouthfuls of sheer decadence, something not for everyday but for rewarding your self and others, for saying thank you, for simply saying I love you, or I love me.... Chocolates are for sharing, and many of these recipes can be made in larger amounts for special occasions, fund raising and presents at Christmas.

Orange Chocolate Truffles

Josceline Dimbleby

Makes: about 20

Preparation time: 30 minutes

Chilling time: 1-2 hours

---

250 g /8 oz /1 ¼ cup 70% dark chocolate or chocolate chips

75 g/ 3 oz unsalted butter, at room temperature

2 tablespoons (2 x 15 ml spoons) double cream

50g/ 2 oz ground almonds

finely grated rind of 1 orange

1 tablespoon (15 ml spoon) drinking chocolate powder

1 teaspoon (5 ml spoon) cinnamon

Break up the chocolate and put it in a bowl set over a pan half-full of very hot water, over a gentle heat; the water should not boil.

Melt the chocolate and then add the butter, a little at a time, and then stir in the cream. Stir until melted and smooth and then remove from the heat and stir in the ground almonds and grated orange rind.

Let the mixture cool and then put it in the fridge until stiff enough to mould into balls. To do this, take up bits of the chocolate mixture with wet hands and lightly pat them on a sheet of greaseproof paper laid on a flat tin or board and return to the fridge until firm. Then mix the chocolate powder and cinnamon together and roll the truffles in this mixture to coat them thoroughly. If possible keep the truffles in the fridge or a cool place until needed.

Bread and Butter Truffles

Paul A Young

Makes: 60 truffles

Preparation time: 30 minutes

Chilling time: 2 hours

You will need: Large flat baking tray, greased

INGREDIENTS FOR THE GANACHE:

250ml / 8 fl oz/ 1 cup whole milk

50g/ 2 oz/ 1/3 cup unrefined golden caster sugar

25g / 1 oz / salted butter

2 thick slices of wholemeal bread torn into pieces.

500g/18 oz / 3 cups milk chocolate broken into small pieces or chocolate chips

INGREDIENTS FOR COATING

400g / 14 oz / 2 1/3 cups tempered* dark chocolate

8 x slices toasted brown bread, whizzed or crushed into breadcrumbs.

INGREDIENTS FOR ROLLING THE TRUFFLES

50g / 2 oz/ ½ cup cocoa powder

In a saucepan, bring the milk, sugar, butter and brown bread to a simmer and whisk until smooth.

Take off the heat and add the milk chocolate pieces whisking until melted and glossy.

Pour into a tray and cool. Refrigerate for 2 hours.

Roll the truffles into even sized balls using your fingers. Dust your fingers with cocoa powder as the ganache is sticky.

Now roll the truffles in tempered dark chocolate (see p 140 for tempered chocolate) then immediately roll through the bread crumbs.

Leave the truffles to set for 5 minutes.

Paul's tips

Store your finished chocolates in air tight containers in a cool dark place. Eat the truffles within seven days.
* For instructions on how to temper chocolate, see p 140

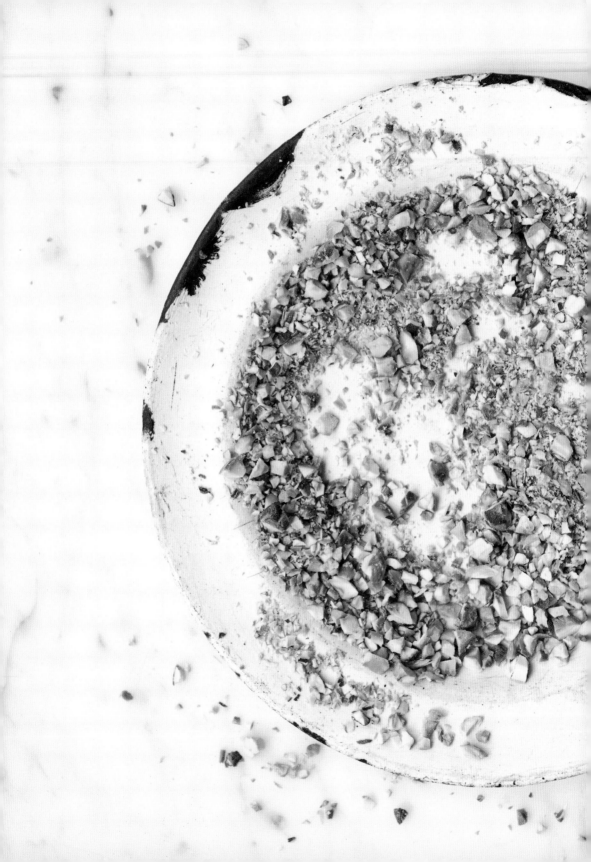

Mango and Saffron Ganache Truffles

Aneesh Popat
Award winning Master Chocolatier

Serves: 8

Preparation time: 30 minutes

Chilling time: 12 hours (overnight) plus another 4 hours the next day.

You will need: A cooking thermometer, a piping bag, a flat tray lined with baking paper

---

50g muscovado sugar

300g mango puree

450g milk chocolate, chopped

4g saffron

cocoa powder for dusting

In a small saucepan lightly toast the saffron to release the flavour. To the saucepan, add the sugar and mango puree. Heat the mixture to 60*C.

Meanwhile, gently melt the milk chocolate over a bain-marie to 45*C.

Pour the mango and saffron mixture over the milk chocolate and gradually blend together using a spatula until a smooth emulsion is formed.

Allow this mixture too cool overnight.

Spoon the ganache into a piping bag with a round tip. Pipe long lines of ganache onto a tray lined with parchment paper and allow this to set for 4 hours.

Use a warm and dry sharp knife to cut the ganache into 4cm logs.

Roll through the cocoa powder and enjoy!

Rose & Pistachio Raw Chocolate

Natasha Corrett

Serves: 6

Preparation time: 30 minutes

Chilling time: 1 hour

You will need: 125cm x 75cm loaf tin lined with baking paper

100g raw cacao butter

25g raw cacao powder

4 tbsp coconut blossom nectar (or agave syrup)

¼ tsp rose water

25g almonds

12g pistachios

Pinch of Himalayan pink salt

Dried rose petals to garnish

Melt the raw cacao butter in a bowl over a pan of simmering water. Once melted, leave to cool for about 5 minutes before mixing through the raw cacao powder with a spoon. Once fully incorporated, add the coconut blossom nectar (or agave) and rose water and whisk into the chocolate so that the syrup doesn't just sink to the bottom of the bowl.

Line either a tin or plate with sides (I used a 7inch long by 3inch wide loaf tin) with baking paper and pour the chocolate in.

Roughly cut up the almonds and pistachios and randomly drop them into the chocolate.

Put the tin/plate into the freezer for 10 minutes then pull out and sprinkle a few more of the nuts onto the top with the rose petals and a sprinkling of pink salt. Then put back into the freezer for 1 hour or until set.

Keep in the freezer or fridge until its ready to be eaten. Enjoy!

Nature's Morganic Superfood Chocolate Bar

Christian Fumic

Serves: 6

Preparation time: 30 minutes

Chilling time: 1 hour

You will need: A food processor, 2 greased flat baking trays, lined with baking paper, a ½ measuring cup and a 1/3 measuring cup.

½ cup of almonds

½ cup of pecans

½ cup of hazelnuts

⅓ cup of Goji berries

⅓ cup dried cranberries

⅓ cup of non-salted pistachio nuts

½ cup of cacao powder

1/3 cup of cacao nibs

1/3 cup of coconut oil

1/3 cup raw coconut nectar

1 tsp chilli powder (optional for the chilli lovers out there)

1 tsp pink Himalayan salt to mix into the pistachio nuts

Boil some water and pour into a large mixing bowl. Place the coconut oil into the bowl of boiling water to slowly melt without reducing its natural goodness.

Roughly chop the nuts, berries and cacao nibs (to your preferred consistency)

Add all the chopped ingredients to the bowl. Mix in the coconut nectar, then divide the mixture in two and spread out evenly.

Cut away the excess baking paper and slice cross and lengthways.

Add your chosen topping, such as pistachio nuts, then cover with clingfilm and place in the fridge for one hour.

Take out and serve – enjoy!

Techniques for ...

How to Caramelise White Chocolate
(see recipe on p50)

Caramelising white chocolate is not a commonly used technique, but is well worth it if you are passionate about baking and chocolate work. The process of caramelisation turns the sugar into caramel, creating a rich toffee akin to dulce de leche, but with cocoa undertones thanks to the presence of cocoa butter. To caramelise white chocolate, use a good quality bar with a high cocoa butter content (about 30% - ideally 32%), as this helps the chocolate to melt and break down evenly. A chocolate of 20% or lower will not melt as evenly, and may dry out.

Preheat the oven to 120°C/gas mark 1/2

Break up the white chocolate into small, evenly sized pieces

Spread out the white chocolate onto a shallow baking tray and place in the oven for 10 minutes

Remove from the oven and stir and spread around the chocolate with a spatula

Repeat this process every 10 minutes for 30-60 minutes, until the white chocolate is deep-golden brown in colour. During this time, the chocolate may turn lumpy and have a 'chalky' appearance - this is normal, so keep going

Once the chocolate has caramelised and has reached the correct consistency, it can be stored in a jar at room temperature for about 2 months

Paul's tips

Caramelised white chocolate is solid at room temperature and can be easily melted and used in any chocolate recipe. Caramelised white chocolate works well with fresh fruit - such as pears. The beauty of caramelised white chocolate is its versatility - you can use it to fill some chocolate shells for a heavenly gift, or simply spread on cake.

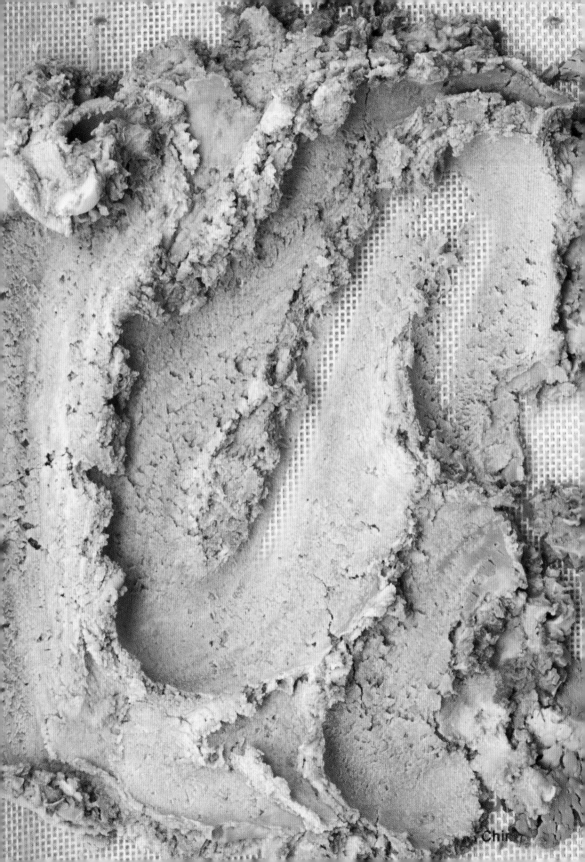

Tempering Dark Chocolate

(see recipe on p128)

400 g (14 oz) chocolate

1 serrated knife

1 kitchen thermometer

1 flexible spatula

1 food processor fitted with a blade attachment.

Tempering by seeding

This tempering method uses the addition of finely chopped pieces, disks or pistoles of chocolate into already-melted chocolate. Adding stable, crystallised chocolate lowers the temperature naturally, enabling regular crystallisation of the chocolate mass. The method is a replacement for using a marble working surface or a cold-water bath.

Chop three quarters of the chocolate (300 g/ 10½ oz) on a chopping board, using a serrated knife. Even better, use couverture chocolate in the form of fèves, buttons or pistoles.

Finely chop the remaining quarter (100 g / 3½ oz) or process it with the blade knife attachment of a food processor.

Place the roughly chopped chocolate in a bowl. Half fill a saucepan with hot water, and put the bowl over it, making sure that the bowl does not touch the bottom of the saucepan. Slowly heat the water, ensuring it does not boil. Alternatively, use a microwave oven if you wish, but in "defrost" position or at 500 W maximum. Stir regularly using a flexible spatula so that the chocolate melts smoothly.

Check the temperature with a thermometer. When it reaches 55°C-58°C (131°F-136°F) for bittersweet/ dark, or 45°C- 50°C (113°F-122°F) for milk or white, remove the chocolate from the bain-marie.

Paul's tips

If the chocolate has attained the right temperature and there are still pieces of unmelted chocolate, remove them before increasing the temperature. If you leave them, the chocolate will thicken very quickly and become sticky because of over-crystallisation.

Set aside one-third of the melted chocolate in a bowl, in a warm place. Add the remaining finely chopped quarter (100 g/ 4 oz) of the chocolate into the remaining two-thirds of the melted chocolate, stirring constantly. Bittersweet/ dark chocolate should reach a temperature of 28°C-29°C (82°F-84°F); milk chocolate should reach 27°C-28°C (81°F-82°F); and white or coloured chocolate should reach 26°C-27°C (79°F-81°F).

Then add the melted chocolate that you have set aside to increase the temperature. Bittersweet/ dark chocolate should reach 31°C-32°C (88°F-90°F); milk chocolate should reach 29°C-30°C (84°F-86°F); an white or coloured chocolate should reach 28°C-29°C (82°F-84°F). Stir until the right temperature is reached.

Sterilizing jars for jam or chutney

(see recipes on p84 and p94)

(see recipes on p84 and p94)

Wash your jars and the lids in hot soapy water, but do not dry them. Instead, leave them to stand upside down on a roasting tray while they're still wet.

Pop the tray of clean, wet jars and lids in to a preheated oven at 160-180ºC for about 15 mins.

Ladle the hot preserve into a heatproof jug to make it easier to transfer the mixture into the hot jars. Be very careful not to touch or get any of the mixture onto the rim of the jars as this could introduce bacteria.

Paul's tips

It's very important to sterilise your jars properly so that you remove bacteria in the jars, which could cause your preserves to spoil. Timing is important because you should put your preserve into a hot jar whilst the preserve itself is still piping hot – it's a good idea so start preparing your jars when your preserve is about 20 mins away from being ready.

Ideally you want to fill the jars not quite to the top, leave about ¼ inch (½ cm) gap at the top between the preserve and the lid.

Whilst everything is still hot, cover the jars with their lids or top with wax paper and a piece of cellophane secured tightly with an elastic band.

Once in sterilised jars like this your preserves should keep for about 6 months in a cool, dark place, but do check the recipe you're using for a more accurate shelf life as some preserves will last longer than others.

Index